Table of Contents

Vice Grip

Understanding and Overcoming Addiction

Tiwayi Mushambi

VICE GRIP: UNDERSTANDING AND OVERCOMING ADDICTION

3

Why I Wrote This Book

I used to think that calling an addiction a disease was a cop-out, used by the weak-willed to excuse their lack of discipline. That was until, in a stunning twist of irony, I got caught up in porn addiction for over 10 years. During that time, I believed that if I developed an iron will, soldiered on in prayer and became accountable to someone, I would be free, but, I was wrong.

In the end, all it took was taking the time to understand my addiction and what feeds it. Addiction is a disease because it is a neurochemical phenomenon that can alter the structure and function of the brain, so willpower alone doesn't cut it. Throw in the guilt and shame that comes with falling off the wagon, along with the temporary dopamine high from another dose, and you have a vicious cycle on your hands.

I realized that aside from my motivations (a temporary high to mask loneliness), there were two things required in order for the addiction to thrive: access(means) and privacy (opportunity). I could have one or the other, but I can't have both. Given how cheap and easily available the internet is, access was unavoidable. But what I could control was the privacy I had to indulge my addiction.

So, I altered my behavior. I stopped taking my phone to the bathroom. I only used headphones if I'm in a room with other people and installed multiple browser extensions that bought me enough time to rethink my next search phrase. Sometimes, I had to take drastic measures, like leaving my headphones and power adapter at home on purpose.

I still occasionally fell off, but I learned to look at it as a learning opportunity and adjusted my routine. Eventually, days became weeks, which became months and then years.

VICE GRIP: UNDERSTANDING AND OVERCOMING ADDICTION

The root causes of addiction are complex and multi-factorial. Some people may even be genetically predisposed to addiction, while others may turn to drugs or alcohol as a way to cope with trauma or stress. Whatever the cause, addiction can have devastating consequences on an individual's physical, financial, emotional, and mental well-being.

For many people struggling with addiction, recovery can seem like an impossible feat. They may feel like they are fighting a losing battle, overwhelmed by the intense cravings and withdrawal symptoms that come with quitting certain substances or behaviors. However, with the right tools, resources, and support, it is possible to overcome even the most entrenched addiction.

This book is a comprehensive guide to overcoming addiction, using decades of research by experts in the field of addiction treatment and recovery. Whether you are battling a drug or alcohol addiction, struggling with a behavioral addiction such as gambling or sex addiction, or simply looking for ways to support a loved one in recovery, this book will provide you with the knowledge and tools you need to succeed.

The first section of the book focuses on understanding addiction - what it is, how it affects the brain, and why it is so difficult to overcome. We will explore the different types of addiction and the risk factors that can contribute to the development of an addiction. I ask you to bear with me as there's a lot of science involved, but I assure you that its easy and necessary to understand first.

The second section of the book provides practical strategies and techniques for overcoming addiction. We will explore various treatment options, including detoxification, therapy, medication-assisted treatment, and support groups. We will also provide tips for managing cravings, coping with stress and anxiety, and building a strong support network.

The third section of the book focuses on maintaining recovery over the long term. We will explore the challenges that can arise during the recovery process, such as triggers and relapse, and provide strategies for overcoming these obstacles. We will also explore the importance of self-care and personal growth in the recovery process and provide tips for maintaining a healthy, fulfilling life in sobriety.

Whether you are just beginning your journey towards recovery or are looking for ways to support a loved one in recovery, this book will provide you with the knowledge, tools, and inspiration you need to succeed. We believe that everyone has the potential to overcome addiction and live a fulfilling, healthy life - and we are here to support you every step of the way.

Understanding Addiction

Humor me for a moment.

Imagine your recovery journey as a climb up a flight of stairs in a skyscraper. The addiction you plan on leaving behind is the ground outside. Every floor has an open window in clear view. Obviously, the higher you go, the more painful the landing if you jump out the window. The hardest part of recovery is the fear of falling if we give in to the urge to defenestrate ourselves, so many jump out at the first floor and never make the climb again.

Addiction is not a choice or a moral failing. It's a chronic condition that affects the brain's reward system and the individual's ability to make sound decisions. Dependence changes the way the brain functions, leading you to prioritize their substance or behavior of choice over everything else in their lives. This can lead to severe consequences, including job loss, relationship breakdowns, financial difficulties, and even death.

Understanding addiction as a disease helps reduce the stigma associated with addiction. Many people still view addiction as a character flaw or weakness, which can prevent you from seeking help. Knowing that addiction is a widespread disease that many have recovered from also helps victims realize that they are not alone and that treatment is available.

Secondly, it's crucial to understand the causes of addiction. Addiction does not have a single, clear cause. Numerous factors can contribute to the development of addiction, including genetics, environment, and mental health. Genetics can play a significant role in addiction, with studies indicating that you with a family history of addiction are more likely to develop addiction than those without. The environment can also play a role, with you experiencing trauma, stress, or peer pressure more susceptible to developing addiction. Mental health conditions can contribute to addiction, with you self-medicating to manage their symptoms.

Understanding the causes of addiction can help you and their loved ones identify when an addiction is developing. It can help them recognize risk factors and take steps to prevent addiction from becoming a severe problem. Additionally, understanding the causes of addiction can shape the approach to treatment, with mental health treatment, family therapy, and support groups all valuable components of addiction recovery.

Thirdly, it's crucial to understand the impact of addiction on you and society as a whole. Addiction can have severe consequences, including job loss, family breakdowns, and financial difficulties. Addiction can also lead to criminal activity, with you turning to theft, drug dealing, or prostitution to fund their addiction. This can, in turn, lead to increased crime rates, putting a strain on law enforcement resources.

In addition to the impact on the individual, addiction also has significant social and economic costs. Treatment and rehabilitation programs can be expensive, putting a strain on public resources. Additionally, addiction can lead to lost productivity in the workforce, lower academic achievements, and increased healthcare costs.

Finally, it's crucial to understand that addiction is treatable. While addiction can be a challenging condition to overcome, with the right support and treatment, you can and do recover. Addiction treatment typically involves a combination of detoxification, therapy, and ongoing support to address the physical and psychological aspects of addiction.

It's essential to understand that addiction recovery is a lifelong process with no quick fix. It requires dedication, patience, and a willingness to embrace change. It may hurt when you fall from the 20th floor of our hypothetical skyscraper, but you are still better off than when you started the climb. It is important to not dwell on the fall, because there's no point in beating yourself up for having a disease. Instead, get back up and continue your recovery.

In conclusion, understanding addiction can encourage more you to seek treatment, and can help them recognize when addiction is developing and take steps to prevent it from becoming a severe problem. Knowing the impact of addiction on you and society can help shape public policy and resources to address this challenging issue. Most importantly, learning that addiction is treatable gives hope to those struggling with addiction that recovery is possible.

The Stages of Addiction

Like all habits, addictions begin as singular actions that use motivation to be repeated consistently until it becomes second nature. Recognizing the various stages of addiction is vital to comprehend how addiction works and how we can prevent it or stop it from developing further.

Experimentation

The experimental stage of addiction can be defined as the initial exposure to the substance or new behavior that is voluntary and motivated by curiosity, peer influence, or other factors. During this stage, you may experiment with drugs or substances, starting with low doses or infrequent use.

The experimental stage of addiction can be a slippery slope that can lead to more severe drug or substance use. Researchers have found that using drugs or substances at a young age can increase the risk of developing addiction later in life. The use of drugs or substances can affect the brain's reward center, which can lead to compulsive drug-seeking behavior in the future.

Studies have shown that young people are more likely to engage in experimental drug use due to various factors like peer pressure, cultural influences, and a lack of knowledge about the dangers of drugs. This is why it is essential to educate young people about the potential dangers of drug use and provide them with the tools necessary to make informed decisions. During the experimental stage of addiction, it is common for you to underestimate the risks involved in drug or substance use. They may believe that they are in control of their drug use and that it will not lead to any significant consequences.

However, this perception can be misleading, and drug use can quickly spiral out of control. Researchers have found that the effects of drugs or substances can vary depending on factors like dosage, the mode of administration, and individual factors like age, mental health, and genetics.

This means that you who engage in experimental drug use can experience a range of effects, including euphoria, impaired judgment, and altered perception. These effects can be enjoyable at first, but the risks involved can increase as the use becomes more frequent or severe. The experimental stage of addiction can also be characterized by the development of tolerance to the drug or substance.

Tolerance is a phenomenon in which you require larger doses of drugs or substances to achieve the same effects. This means that you who engage in experimental drug use may continue to increase their dosage as they develop tolerance, leading to greater risks of addiction, overdose, or other adverse effects. Preventing the experimental stage of addiction is a crucial step in reducing the risks of addiction later in life.

Researchers have found that you who delay their initiation of drug or substance use are less likely to develop addiction later in life. This is why it is essential to provide young people with support and education that can help them make informed decisions about drug use.

It is also essential to address the root causes of drug use, such as peer pressure, stress, or mental health issues. Providing young people with healthy coping mechanisms and support systems can reduce the risks of drug use and addiction. In conclusion, the experimental stage of addiction is a critical phase of drug or substance use that can lead to greater risks of addiction, tolerance, and adverse effects.

Educating young people about the potential dangers of drug use, providing them with support and healthy coping mechanisms, and addressing the root causes of drug use can reduce the risks of addiction and help prevent drug-related harm.

Regular Use

While the causes of addiction may vary from person to person, the regular use stage of addiction is a critical phase that requires attention and intervention. It is the phase in which an individual has developed a regular pattern of substance use. At this stage, the individual may begin to feel a sense of comfort and familiarity with the substance, leading to a psychological and sometimes physical dependence.

During the regular use stage, the individual may begin to develop routines around their drug use, such as using a particular substance at a certain time of day, in a specific location, or with a group of people. The individual may also experience tolerance, a process in which the body adapts to the substance and requires more of it to achieve the desired effect.

Tolerance is a significant risk factor for overdose and other adverse health effects of substance use. Underlying Factors that Contribute to the Regular Use Stage of Addiction The regular use stage of addiction may be influenced by a range of factors, including psychological, environmental, and genetic factors. Some of the key factors that contribute to this stage of addiction include:

Genetics: Research has shown that genes play a significant role in addiction. You with a family history of substance use disorders may be more susceptible to developing addiction themselves.

Environment: Environmental factors such as peer pressure, stress, trauma, and availability of substances may also contribute to the regular use stage of addiction.

Mental Health: You with underlying mental health disorders, such as depression, anxiety, or ADHD, may use substances to self-medicate, leading to the regular use stage of addiction.

Age of Onset: The age at which you begin using substances is also a risk factor for the regular use stage of addiction. You who begin using substances at an early age may be more prone to developing an addiction later in life.

Consequences of the Regular Use Stage of Addiction

Some of the possible consequences of the regular use stage of addiction include:

Physical Health Problems: Substance use can have a range of adverse physical health effects, such as liver damage, heart disease, lung cancer, and more.

Mental Health Problems: Substance use can also lead to mental health problems such as depression, anxiety, substance-induced psychosis, and personality disorders.

Loss of Relationships: The regular use stage of addiction can also have a significant impact on the individual's relationships. They may begin to experience strain in their relationships with family members, friends, and partners, leading to feelings of isolation and loneliness.

Legal Issues: Substance use can lead to legal problems; such as arrests for drug possession or driving under the influence.

Financial Problems: Substance use can also lead to financial problems as you may begin to prioritize their drug use over financial responsibilities such as rent, bills, and food.

Seeking Help for the Regular Use Stage of Addiction

The first step is recognizing that there is a problem and seeking help. Some of the options available for seeking help at this stage include:

Detox and Rehabilitation Programs

Detox and rehabilitation programs offer a range of services, including medical detox, counseling, and behavioral therapies to help you overcome addiction.

Mutual Support Groups

Mutual support groups, such as Alcoholics Anonymous, Narcotics Anonymous, and SMART Recovery, provide a supportive community for you in recovery.

Therapy

Individual and group therapy can also be beneficial for you in the regular use stage of addiction, helping them identify the underlying causes of their addiction and develop coping skills.

Conclusion

While seeking help may seem like a daunting task, there are a range of options available to support you through the recovery process. By recognizing the problem and seeking help, you can take control of their addiction and improve their quality of life.

Bingeing

The bingeing stage of addiction is often the point at which many you begin to experience significant negative consequences related to their substance use or compulsive behavior. This stage is characterized by a period of intense, excessive consumption or engagement with the substance or behavior, often far beyond the average or recommended dosage or frequency.

This behavior can lead to a range of physical, psychological, and social problems for you struggling with addiction. One of the primary reasons that bingeing can be so dangerous and damaging is that it often reflects a loss of control over the substance or behavior. Once an individual has crossed the threshold from moderate or occasional use into the territory of bingeing, it can be much harder to regulate or limit their consumption.

This can be due to a range of factors, including the addictive effects of the substance or behavior, cravings or withdrawal symptoms, social pressures or stressors, or underlying mental health issues. For example, you who struggle with binge drinking may find that they are unable to stop or moderate their alcohol use once they have started drinking. This may lead to dangerous levels of intoxication, impaired judgment and decision-making, and a range of physical and psychological health consequences.

Similarly, you who are addicted to gambling may go into a state of compulsive gambling, spending increasing amounts of money and time on their habit in order to chase the high or win back their losses. The effects of bingeing on the body can be varied and significant.

Depending on the substance or behavior in question, you may experience a range of physical symptoms, including nausea, vomiting, dizziness, tremors, seizures, or increased heart rate and blood pressure. Long-term bingeing behavior can also lead to serious health problems, including liver damage, heart disease, chronic pain, or neuropathy.

Bingeing can also have significant psychological effects, both in the short and long-term. In the immediate aftermath of a binge, you may feel extreme euphoria or pleasure, followed by a period of intense emotional or psychological distress. This may include feelings of shame, guilt, anxiety, or depression, combined with physical symptoms such as fatigue or insomnia.

Over time, the psychological impact of bingeing can become even more pronounced. You struggling with addiction may experience changes in their brain chemistry or structure, leading to greater difficulty regulating their emotions or making good decisions. They may also develop a range of co-occurring mental health issues, such as anxiety or depression, that can further interfere with their ability to cope with stress or life events.

The social consequences of bingeing are also significant and can have long-lasting effects on you' lives. Bingeing may lead to strained relationships with friends and family, as well as problems at work or school. You may become isolated or withdraw from social activities, leading to feelings of loneliness or alienation. In some cases, you may become involved in criminal activity or experience legal problems related to their substance use or behavior.

Despite the significant negative consequences associated with bingeing, many you struggling with addiction find it difficult to stop or moderate their behavior. This may be due to the addictive effects of the substance or behavior, as well as other psychological or social factors that contribute to the development and maintenance of addiction.

Treatment for bingeing as part of the addiction process can be complex and may involve a combination of behavioral and medical interventions. Depending on the nature of the addiction and the individual's specific needs, treatment may involve substance abuse counseling, therapy, or medication-assisted treatment to help manage withdrawal symptoms or cravings.

In some cases, residential or inpatient treatment may be necessary to provide a safe and supportive environment for you to detox and begin their recovery journey. Ultimately, the bingeing stage of addiction is a critical point at which you may be most in need of support and intervention.

By recognizing the signs and symptoms of bingeing and seeking help early, you struggling with addiction can take steps towards managing their behavior and improving their health and well-being.

Dependence

At this stage, the individual's body has become used to the presence of substances or the release of dopamine. This leads to physical withdrawal symptoms when they stop using or erratic behavior. Dependence is characterized by the experience of various symptoms that occur because of stopping. One of the primary symptoms of dependence is physical withdrawal. This is an experience that occurs when an individual stops using the drug.

Withdrawal can manifest in various ways, including sweating, shaking, agitation, insomnia, nausea, and muscle aches. Withdrawal symptoms generally signal that the individual has become physically dependent on the substance, and their body has become used to its presence. Another symptom of dependence is tolerance. Tolerance is defined as the need for higher doses of a drug to achieve the desired effect.

This happens because the body becomes used to the drug's presence and requires more of it to get the desired effect. Tolerance makes it easier to develop addiction, as the individual needs more of the drug to get the same effect. Tolerance is also one of the leading causes of overdose, as you consume higher and higher amounts of the drug to achieve the desired effect.

Another symptom of dependence is craving. Craving is an intense desire to consume drugs or alcohol. It's generally characterized by an intense feeling that compels the individual to use again. Cravings can be triggered by various factors, including stress, social situations, or certain stimuli. Dependence is most often characterized by these physical symptoms, but there are other symptoms that can be psychological in nature as well. Many you report feeling anxious, depressed, or irritable at this stage. Mood swings are quite common, and you may find that they have changed in personality or behavior.

This often contributes to social difficulties and strains relationships. In conclusion, dependence is a significant stage in the progression of addiction. At this stage, you have developed physical dependence and experience different withdrawal symptoms when they stop using drugs or alcohol.

Tolerance and cravings are other symptoms of dependence and make it easier for an individual to progress to drug addiction. Addiction is a chronic disease that requires immediate treatment, and the earlier it's identified, the more likely the individual is to avoid the negative consequences of drug or alcohol abuse. Treatment options for addiction often include medications, behavior therapy, and vocational counseling.

Addiction

During the addiction stage, substance use becomes the individual's primary focus, and they are willing to go to great lengths to indulge or use their vice of choice. They may spend most or all of their money on drugs, compromise personal values and morality to get the substance, and lose sight of what is important in their life.

They may also start to experience physical and psychological symptoms of addiction, such as tolerance, withdrawal, and cravings. At this stage, the individual's substance use has become a compulsive behavior that they cannot control. Intense cravings for the substance appear, which can lead to the use of more drugs or alcohol than intended. They may also experience withdrawal symptoms when the drug is not available, such as nausea, vomiting, headaches, irritability, and anxiety. These symptoms often lead to further drug use to relieve the discomfort, and the cycle of addiction continues.

In addition to physical symptoms, you in the addiction stage also experience psychological symptoms of addiction. They may feel a sense of hopelessness and despair over their inability to control their drug use. They may also suffer from depression, anxiety, and other mental health problems as a result of their addiction.

These psychological symptoms can also lead to more drug use as the person tries to numb their emotions. The addiction stage is not just detrimental to the individual's physical and mental health, but also to their relationships and overall quality of life. They may become isolated as they prioritize substance use over spending time with friends and family.

It is important to note that the addiction stage is not a point of no return. Recovery is possible, but it requires the individual to acknowledge their addiction and seek help. Treatment for addiction typically involves a range of approaches, such as behavioral therapy, medication-assisted treatment, and support groups.

The most effective approach to treatment varies from person to person, depending on their individual needs and circumstances. In conclusion, addiction is a complex and chronic illness that can manifest in various stages. The addiction stage is the most severe stage of addiction, characterized by physical and psychological dependence on a substance. At this stage, the individual's life is controlled by their addiction, and they may experience intense cravings and withdrawal symptoms. Recovery is possible, but it requires the individual to seek help and use the following.

The Role Of Willpower

As I stated in this book's introduction, there are three things required for an addiction to take a hold of your life:

- Motivation;
- Means and
- Opportunity

In some cases, recovery involves being deprived of the means and opportunity to indulge your vices by checking into rehab. In others, you become a part of a community where you shift your motives in the hopes that you will self-regulate when the means and opportunity pop up.

How many people do you hear or read about, who check into rehab, only to relapse the moment they get back? While addiction is caused by a neurochemical dependency, it does not take willpower out of the equation. The problem is not that addicts don't have the willpower to overcome their brain's rewiring, the problem is that they are pointing their willpower in the wrong direction.

If you are always face to face with your vice, no amount of mental fortitude can keep you away. Instead, you are supposed to use willpower in order to adhere to a new set of rules that keep you away from your triggers. Stay away from the casinos; change your circle of friends; refrain from typing the letter 'X' in your search bar. Exercising your willpower in adhering to rules is a lot easier than using it to resist temptation.

Of course, willpower alone is rarely enough to overcome addiction. Recovery often requires a combination of strategies and support, such as therapy, medication, and lifestyle changes. However, willpower can be an instrumental tool in the recovery process, providing a foundation of strength and resilience that can help you make positive changes and break free from the cycle of addiction.

Addiction is not just a physical problem – it also has psychological and emotional components that can be difficult to overcome. For those struggling with addiction, willpower can be an integral tool in breaking the cycle of addiction and creating positive change. Willpower is the ability to resist short-term temptations and desires in order to make better long-term decisions. It involves self-control and self-discipline, and is a crucial component of behavioral change.

In the context of addiction, willpower involves resisting the urge to engage in addictive behaviors, even when faced with triggers or tempting situations. This requires a great deal of inner strength and determination, as well as the ability to stay focused on long-term goals and desired outcomes. One of the reasons that willpower is so important in overcoming addiction is that it allows you to take control of their actions and decisions.

When someone is in the grips of addiction, their behavior is often dictated by the substance or behavior they are addicted to. They may feel powerless to resist the urge to drink, use drugs, or engage in other behaviors that they know are harmful to themselves and those around them. With willpower, however, an individual can recognize the negative impact of addiction on their life and make a conscious decision to change.

This may involve setting specific goals, such as reducing or quitting drug use, or adopting new habits and routines that support a healthier lifestyle. By taking control of their behavior, you can regain a sense of agency and personal responsibility. Another important role of willpower in overcoming addiction is that it helps you cope with stress and other triggers that may lead to relapse. Addiction often stems from a desire to numb feelings of anxiety, depression, or other negative emotions.

By building up their willpower, you can learn to manage these emotions in healthier ways, such as through exercise, journaling, or seeking support from friends and family. In addition, willpower can help you stay committed to long-term goals and resist the temptation to give up when faced with setbacks or obstacles.

Recovery from addiction is rarely a linear process and often involves ups and downs. It can be difficult to stay motivated and on track when progress is slow or when faced with unexpected challenges. With willpower, however, you can stay focused on their ultimate goals and maintain a sense of determination even in the face of adversity.

One way to build willpower is through mindfulness practices, such as meditation and mindful breathing. These practices can help you cultivate a greater sense of self-awareness and self-control, allowing them to better resist cravings and make healthier choices.

Regular exercise can also be an effective way to build willpower, as it requires discipline and persistence over time. Seeking support from others can also be crucial in building willpower and overcoming addiction. This may involve confiding in friends and family members, joining a support group, or working with a therapist or addiction specialist. Having a strong support network can provide you with the encouragement and accountability they need to stay committed to their recovery goals. In conclusion, willpower is a vital tool in overcoming addiction. It requires a great deal of inner strength and determination, but can help you take control of their behavior, manage triggers and stressors, stay committed to long-term goals, and break the cycle of addiction.

While willpower alone may not be enough to achieve full recovery, it can provide a foundation of strength that can support you as they work towards a healthier, more fulfilling life. With the right strategies and support in place, anyone can tap into their willpower and take the first steps towards recovery.

The Importance of Support Systems

The people who are hurt the most by your addiction are also the same people who can help you break free. That is why making amends is a vital step in most addiction recovery programs. It doesn't matter if you stole money from their wallet, gambled away their house or missed out on half their life. You have to earn their forgiveness and trust, because these people will form your close-knit support system and keep you accountable.

Addiction not only affects the person suffering from it, but it also impacts their relationships, career, and overall quality of life. While there are many effective treatments for addiction, one of the most critical components of successful recovery is having a strong support system.

Your support system is a network of people who will offer encouragement, guidance, and emotional support to you while you grapple with addiction. It can consist of family members, friends, therapists, support groups, or any combination of these you need.

The importance of having a support system in overcoming addiction cannot be overstated. Having a supportive network that can offer guidance, advice, and encouragement can greatly increase your chances of long-term recovery. One of the primary benefits of a support system is that it provides you with a sense of community and connection. Addiction can be an isolating disease, and many people who suffer from it often feel alone and disconnected from others.

This sense of isolation can make it difficult for you to seek help or stay committed to treatment. However, with the support of a community, you can feel more motivated to seek help and persist through the difficulties of recovery.

Moreover, a support system can help you with addiction to feel more accountable and responsible for your actions. Having people in your life who know about your addiction and are invested in your recovery can help you become more committed to changing your behavior and achieving recovery goals. Accountability is a vital component of recovery as it can help you to be more honest with yourself and others about their challenges and progress.

Another critical component that support systems offer is that they can provide you with practical help to overcome addiction. For example, family members or friends can help with the execution of lifestyle changes that are essential to recovery. Healthier eating habits, exercise, and removing triggers from the person's everyday life are all significant goals that can be more easily accomplished with the support of others.

A support system can also offer stability to you in recovery by ensuring that you are not alone in your journey and have help managing triggers and moments of need. They also enable you to process difficult emotions and experiences that may have led to addiction. It is not uncommon for people struggling with addiction to have experienced significant trauma or hardship in their lives.

The emotional support provided by a support system can help people in recovery to process these experiences and emotions in a safe and supportive environment. Therapists, support groups, and peers can help you work through their emotions and turn to healthier coping mechanisms rather than relying on their addiction to manage these feelings.

Finally, a support system can offer encouragement and motivation to you when you are struggling in recovery. Addiction recovery can be a long and challenging journey, and many people experience setbacks or lapses throughout the process. A supportive community can provide you with the courage and strength to keep pushing forward, even in the most challenging moments.

Moreover, a support system can help you set achievable goals and milestones to work toward, and they will be there to celebrate those milestones with you, creating a strong positive association.

In short, support systems provide you with a sense of community, accountability, practical help, emotional support, and encouragement that are essential to achieving long-term recovery success. Addiction is often a lonely and isolating journey, but with the support of family, friends, therapists, and support groups, you can find the strength and motivation to overcome their addiction and live a healthier, happier life.

Do not isolate yourself in shame. Educate your loved ones on the disease if you have to. It is important to surround yourself with people that love you and are invested in your success.

The Steps Towards Recovery

The first step towards recovery from addiction is admitting there is a problem. This means acknowledging that the addiction is negatively impacting their life and relationships. This can be a difficult step as addicts often experience denial and may blame others or external circumstances for their problems. Denial may stem from feelings of guilt, shame, fear of judgment, or a lack of awareness of the problem. However, admitting the problem is a crucial step in acknowledging that recovery is necessary.

The next step is to seek professional help. Addiction treatment programs and support groups provide assistance in recovery from addiction. Treatment options include inpatient and outpatient drug rehabilitation centers, counseling services, and medication-assisted treatment. The focus of addiction treatment is to help the individual abstain from drugs and learn coping mechanisms and skills for a successful life in recovery.

Support groups provide a safe environment for you in recovery to share experiences, ideas, and encouragement with others who have had similar struggles. Support groups can be online or in-person and provide an opportunity for you in recovery to form strong bonds with others. After seeking professional help and support, the next step is to establish a support network.

In the previous chapter, we learned that a support network is made up of family, friends, and other you who are dedicated to helping the person in recovery stay sober. These people offer assistance with everyday tasks, help keep the person in recovery accountable, and provide encouragement and motivation.

You should also adopt healthy habits such as regular exercise, a balanced diet, good sleep and hygiene. Exercise releases endorphins, which are natural mood enhancers, that help manage stress. A balanced diet provides proper nutrition, which can help to prevent and manage diseases such as obesity, diabetes, and heart disease.

Sleep hygiene is the practice of creating healthy habits for sleeping, such as establishing a regular schedule, adopting a consistent bedtime routine, and creating a comfortable sleeping environment. These healthy habits can reduce stress, improve mood, and promote a healthy lifestyle.

You must also identify and address underlying issues or triggers that contribute to your addiction. These may include mental health conditions, such as depression and anxiety, past trauma, or stressful environments. A holistic approach to addiction treatment considers the whole person, not just the addiction. It is important to address any underlying issues to ensure a lasting recovery.

In addition to addressing underlying issues and triggers, you must also develop healthy coping mechanisms to manage stress and emotions in a healthy way. Instead of turning to drugs to cope, recovering you should adopt healthy coping mechanisms such as physical exercise, meditation or mindfulness practices, hobbies, or hobbies such as gardening, knitting, reading, or doing other creative activities.

During the recovery process, it is crucial to maintain a positive outlook and focus on progress rather than perfection. Recovery is not a quick process and relapses can occur. It is important to remember that setbacks do not define the person in recovery and that each day is a new opportunity to make progress towards an addiction-free lifestyle. Maintaining positive attitudes, self-forgiveness, and compassion can have a positive impact on the recovery process by building resilience and promoting a positive outlook on life.

Finally, it may be necessary to make amends, seek forgiveness, and rebuild trust with those who were hurt by their addiction. This process can be difficult but is an important step towards healing and rebuilding relationships that may have been damaged.

SUMMARY

Seeking professional help, building a support network, and establishing healthy habits are crucial steps in the process. Identifying and addressing underlying issues, developing healthy coping mechanisms, and maintaining positivity and focus on progress rather than perfection can also greatly benefit the recovery process. Finally, reconnecting with family and loved ones can help rebuild relationships that may have been damaged. Recovery is a difficult but rewarding journey towards a new, productive, and addiction-free lifestyle.

The Ongoing Battle

Taking things one day at a time can give people the opportunity to focus on their recovery efforts for a single day rather than thinking about the whole process of quitting an addiction. You can't jump from zero to 100 days sober. It's an accumulation of taking things a day at a time. A string of "No"s joined together by exercising willpower to stick to new patterns of behavior. This allows you to remain positive about your progress, which is essential for long-term success.

One of the ways to approach addiction recovery one day at a time is by setting achievable short-term goals. Instead of focusing on a long-term goal such as staying sober for the rest of their lives, people can focus on shorter achievable tasks such as not drinking or using drugs for the next 24 hours.

This helps to keep a person focused on the small steps they need to take every day rather than getting caught up in the overwhelming idea of quitting an addiction entirely. By achieving these mini-goals, people begin to build confidence and ultimately increase their chances of achieving their overall goal of long-term recovery.

Taking one day at a time also allows you to stay in the present moment. Trying to change the past or worrying about the future can lead to stress and anxiety that can ultimately trigger the addictive behavior. Instead, you should focus your energy on controlling your addiction in the present moment. This can help to manage the overwhelming emotions that can come with addiction recovery, such as feelings of guilt, shame, and regret. By keeping focus on the present, people are better equipped to handle the emotions that arise as a part of the recovery process.

Another benefit of taking addiction recovery one day at a time is the opportunity to learn new habits and coping mechanisms. Addiction is often a response to stress or trauma, and people who struggle with addiction often lack healthy coping mechanisms to deal with their emotional struggles.

By focusing on recovery one day at a time, people can develop new, healthy habits that will support them in staying sober. These habits can include things like meditation, exercise, or therapy. By working on these habits one day at a time, people can slowly build new coping mechanisms that will help them avoid the addictive behaviors that once ruled their lives.

One of the biggest challenges of addiction recovery is dealing with triggers. Triggers are situations, events, or people that can set off cravings and lead to a relapse. When people take their recovery one day at a time, they can focus on managing these triggers one at a time. This can help to break the cycle of addictive behavior and slowly build resistance to triggers over time. By focusing on one trigger at a time, people can learn to identify and manage problematic situations before they spiral out of control.

One of the major drawbacks to traditional approaches to addiction recovery is the focus on the long-term goal rather than the journey. This can lead to feelings of overwhelm that can lead to relapse and discouragement. By taking things one day at a time, people can build confidence and gain a sense of accomplishment as they achieve their daily goals. This momentum can be a powerful motivator in the recovery process.

Although the road to recovery can be long and difficult, taking things one day at a time can make the process much more manageable. By focusing on short-term achievable goals, developing healthy habits, managing triggers, and staying in the present moment, you can build the foundation for long-term addiction recovery success. By taking it one day at a time, people can focus on the small things they can do each day to lead a healthier and happier life.

Hope For The Future

One of the key elements of successful recovery from addiction is hope. Hope is the belief that one can overcome their addiction and achieve a better life. Hope provides motivation and inspiration to you in recovery and helps them to persevere through difficult times. In this essay, I will explore the importance of hope in recovery from addiction and the ways in which you can keep hope alive during the recovery process.

The Importance of Hope in Recovery

Hope is an essential component of recovery from addiction, and for good reason. Studies have shown that hope is closely linked to positive outcomes in recovery, including decreased substance use, improved mental health, and overall well-being. When you have hope, you are more motivated to continue their recovery journey, even when faced with challenges and setbacks.

Hope also provides you in recovery with a sense of purpose and direction. It gives them something to work towards and strive for in their lives. Without hope, you may struggle to find meaning in their recovery and may be more likely to give up on your journey towards sobriety. Furthermore, hope helps you to develop a positive mindset.

When you have hope, you are more likely to approach challenges with a positive attitude and see setbacks as opportunities for growth and learning. This positive attitude can help you to remain resilient and persevere through the tough times that often accompany recovery from addiction.

Ways to Keep Hope Alive

Keeping hope alive is essential during the recovery process. Here are some ways that you can maintain a sense of hope during their journey towards sobriety.

Set small goals. Setting small goals is a great way to keep hope alive during the recovery process. These goals should be achievable and aligned with the individual's overall recovery plan. When you accomplish these goals, you feel a sense of accomplishment and progress towards their ultimate goal of long-term sobriety. Celebrating these small victories can help you to maintain hope and momentum throughout their recovery journey.

Build a support system. A strong support system is crucial for you in recovery to maintain hope and motivation throughout their journey. This support system can include friends, family members, and professionals such as therapists and support group members. Having a support system in place helps you to feel connected and supported, which can help boost their sense of hope and remind them that you are not alone in their recovery journey.

Practice self-care. Self-care is an essential component of maintaining hope during the recovery process. Practicing self-care can help you to take care of themselves physically, emotionally, and mentally. This includes getting enough sleep, exercising regularly, eating a healthy diet, and engaging in activities that bring joy and fulfillment.

When you take care of themselves, you feel better overall, which can help them to maintain hope and make progress towards their recovery goals.

Stay optimistic. Remaining optimistic is crucial for maintaining hope during the recovery process. It can be easy to get bogged down by setbacks and challenges, but you who stay optimistic are more likely to persevere through the tough times. This can be achieved by focusing on the positives, practicing gratitude, and remaining hopeful about the future.

Seek help when needed. Finally, seeking help when needed is essential for you in recovery to maintain hope. This may include seeking out therapy or support group meetings, reaching out to friends and family members, or enlisting the help of a sober companion. When you feel overwhelmed or hopeless, seeking help can provide them with the support and guidance you need to stay on track towards their recovery goals.

Conclusion

Hope is a crucial component of successful recovery from addiction. You who maintain a sense of hope throughout their recovery journey are more likely to meet their goals and achieve long-term sobriety. By setting small goals, building a support system, practicing self-care, staying optimistic, and seeking help when needed, you in recovery can keep hope alive and continue to persevere through the challenges of recovery.

Where To Get Help

Not everyone has a family or a support system ready to go when they decide to get clean. It is important to help those people and let them know that there's still hope. Here are some of the places where someone struggling with addiction can find help:

Treatment centers

Treatment centers are designed specifically to help those struggling with addiction. They offer a range of services, including detox, therapy, and support groups. Treatment centers can be residential or outpatient, depending on the individual's needs and preferences.

Residential treatment centers are often recommended for those with severe addictions or who have been unsuccessful in other treatment options. These centers offer 24-hour care and support, providing a safe and structured environment for recovery. Outpatient treatment centers allow you to receive treatment on a part-time basis, allowing them to continue with certain aspects of their life, such as work or school.

Support groups

Support groups are another valuable resource for those struggling with addiction. They provide a safe and supportive environment for you to share their experiences and receive encouragement from others who are going through similar challenges. There are many different types of support groups available, including 12-step programs, faith-based groups, and more.

12-step programs, such as Alcoholics Anonymous and Narcotics Anonymous, are some of the most well-known support groups. These programs are based on the principles of admitting powerlessness over addiction and surrendering to a higher power for help. They also emphasize the importance of fellowship and support from others in recovery.

There are also non-12-step support groups such as Smart Recovery, which focuses on teaching you practical skills to overcome addiction. Faith-based support groups, such as Celebrate Recovery, combine a spiritual component with traditional addiction treatment methods.

Counseling and therapy

Online counseling sites, like Better Help, have made it easier for people who would otherwise have not had access to traditional therapy.

Counseling and therapy can be incredibly helpful for those struggling with addiction. These services can help you identify and address the underlying issues that contribute to their addiction, such as trauma, anxiety, or depression. They also provide support in developing healthy coping mechanisms and preventing future relapse.

There are many different types of counseling and therapy available, including cognitive-behavioral therapy (CBT), dialectical behavior therapy (DBT), and motivational interviewing (MI). You can work with a licensed therapist or counselor individually or participate in group therapy sessions.

Medical professionals

Medical professionals, such as doctors and psychiatrists, can play an important role in addiction recovery. They can help manage withdrawal symptoms, provide medication-assisted treatment (MAT), and address any co-occurring mental health conditions.

MAT involves the use of medications, such as methadone or buprenorphine, to help manage withdrawal symptoms and cravings. It can be incredibly helpful for those struggling with opioid addiction.

Medical professionals can also diagnose and treat any mental health conditions, such as depression or anxiety, which often co-occur with addiction.

Friends and family

Friends and family members can provide invaluable support to those struggling with addiction. They can provide encouragement, offer help with daily responsibilities, and be a listening ear when needed.

It's important to note that friends and family members may also need support themselves. Addiction can be incredibly challenging for loved ones to navigate, and they may need to seek counseling or join a support group to manage their own emotions and stress.

Online resources

Online resources, such as websites, forums, and educational materials, can also be helpful for those struggling with addiction. These resources can provide information on addiction and its treatment, as well as support from peers and professionals.

For example, the National Institute on Drug Abuse (NIDA) offers a wealth of information on addiction and its treatment. The Substance Abuse and Mental Health Services Administration (SAMHSA) also provides a directory of treatment centers and support groups across the country.

There are also many online forums and communities, such as SoberRecovery and AddictionCenter, where you can receive support and guidance from others in recovery.

In conclusion, addiction is a challenging disease that often requires professional help to overcome. From treatment centers to support groups to medical professionals, there are many resources available to those struggling with addiction. It's important to remember that recovery is a journey, and it may take time and multiple attempts to achieve lasting sobriety. However, with the right support and resources, recovery is within reach.

Bonus: Motivation for Willpower

"Knowing is not enough; we must apply. Willing is not enough: we must do. "

- Bruce Lee

Without discipline, all the motivational teachings and time management strategies in the world will never be effective. You can keep playing around with words like 'change', 'strive', 'courage', 'no excuses', 'desire to improve', 'be persistent' and 'goal setting' all you want. It is easy to utter these words, but it is an arduous task to get yourself to do it.

In short, it is easier said than done. Don't get me wrong; motivation is a wonderful thing. It is what gets us going in the first place, but self-discipline is the only thing that will keep us going once the excitement dries up. In my search for knowledge, I've attended seminars, sermons and workshops about anything and everything more times than I'd like to count.

At some point, I began to realize that the ones who benefited the most from these meetings were not those who clapped the most, shouted the loudest "Amen" or grinned from ear to ear when the speaker made a joke, but those who continued to do what they were taught long after the fact.

The hard truth is — half of the time — all of us know or have an idea of what we should do to improve the areas of our lives that we are not satisfied with. Having financial problems? Increase your sources of income, save more, spend less and invest the rest. Weight issues? Go on a diet, exercise and drink lots of water. Loneliness? Become a friend in order to have friends.

I don't mean to underrate what are in fact serious problems that people struggle with on a regular basis, but even the tallest of mountains can be climbed over time. Of course, the time it takes to overcome that mountain differs from person to person, but it can be done nonetheless. Some are born great, some achieve greatness, and some have greatness thrust upon them. That's not just a Shakespeare quote, but a truth about the way the world works. There's also no reason why you cannot be any of the three.

Let's not be naïve, though. Genetics, family\educational background and relationships do give some people a distinct advantage over others, but it is your choice to use that as a crutch for the rest of your life or not.

Countless books, articles and videos have provided solutions (some even supported by science) to our biggest problems and more. I'm sure a lot of us have even come across some 'helpful' quotes on the internet and social platforms. My favorites so far are, "If you don't like where you are then you should move; you're not a tree." and "When life gives you lemons, make grape juice. Then sit back and watch as the world wonders how you did it."

It doesn't matter if you're ready to charge Hell with a water pistol after a riveting presentation; what matters is the energy you put into making it a reality, even when you don't feel like it. Most people, if motivated enough, go as far as BEGINNING to do what needs to be done. They get a gym membership, open a savings account, or enroll in a class, but the real change lies in CONTINUING to do what is necessary.

We live in a lightning-fast information age, and there is no doubt the knowledge that empowers us to succeed in various spheres of our lives is readily available. However, it's not the truth that we know that sets us free, but the truth that we know and apply. Positive change is intentional, and self-discipline allows us to take our lives off auto-pilot and steer towards continuous improvement.

Most of the troubles that plague modern individuals in our society — addiction, abuse, crime, domestic violence, sexually transmitted diseases, unwanted pregnancies, prejudice, financial debt, failure at school and work, obesity — have some degree of self-control failure as a central aspect. We are too busy letting ourselves go, falling for the wrong people or getting hooked on something bad or counterproductive to take responsibility and grow as individuals. This is (mostly) a free world, but the word "freedom" has shifted its meaning from "liberty" to "casting off restraint".

However, contrary to popular belief, self-discipline does not mean being hard on yourself, or having a restrictive lifestyle. It means self-control, which is a result of inner strength, and it is vital for success in today's world. Delayed gratification, focus, work ethic, perseverance, commitment and a standard of excellence are the staples of a successful person.

Theodore Bryant, a Human Behavior Specialist, says that there is a part of each and every one of us that resists change. He called this part 'Mr. Hyde'. To avoid self-discipline, Hyde uses tactics such as:

cynicism;

negativism;

defeatism;

escapism and

delay-ism

Fear of failure, success (that's right), risks, rejection and mediocrity keeps a lot of us from stepping out of our comfort zones to embrace discipline. Self-discipline is a skill that can be learned, and I invite you to come on this journey with me. Discover your true potential and awaken the giant inside of you (this time, for real).

Enjoy your reading. This will be the first of many victories for your life.

HABITS AND ADDICTIONS

"I fear not the man who has practiced 10,000 kicks once, but i fear the man who has practiced one kick 10,000 times. "

- Bruce Lee

When you fold your arms, have you ever consciously thought about which arm to cross over the other? No? The next time you do fold your arms, take note of how your arms are positioned. This is how you fold your arms every time, whether you are aware of it or not. It's how you naturally do it, and you are comfortable with it.

Now try folding your arms the opposite way; if your right arm normally crosses over your left, cross your left over your right and vice versa. It feels awkward doesn't it? That's because you're not used to it. But if you take a minute of your time every day to practice doing so, in about three weeks you will automatically fold your arms in the way that felt awkward before. This is the power of habit.

A bad habit, if left unchecked, transforms into an addiction. Addictions negatively affect our physical, mental and emotional well-being. They rob us of the energy we were supposed to direct to achieving goals and warp our priorities.

I once read about a retired war veteran who became addicted to narcotic drugs. In order to kick the habit, he locked himself up in a room for three weeks and came out sober. Not everyone can take such drastic measures ('cold turkey' method) to seize back control over their lives, but Steve Pavlina, author of Personal Development For Smart People, says that the solution is to diagnose the bad habit that is hurting you and devise a new habit to replace it, de-conditioning the old habit and installing the new one. Here is his story:

VICE GRIP: UNDERSTANDING AND OVERCOMING ADDICTION

"In January 1991, my life was going downhill fast. I'd just been arrested for felony grand theft after a few prior arrests for misdemeanors. I got expelled from college because I ditched most of my classes. I played video games for up to 18 hours at a time. I'd fallen into a pattern of self-destructive, out-of-control behavior.

I didn't know how at the time, but I decided I had to make some serious changes. I really didn't want to spend my adult years wearing orange pajamas. I began listening to personal development audio programs, and I liked the positive messages they shared. Sometimes I listened to them for 2-3 hours per day.

This had a major effect on my attitude, thoughts, and beliefs. I gradually began setting goals, working on my self-discipline, and overcoming bad habits.

Soon I started over at a new university. Thanks to all this positive conditioning, I was able to take triple the normal course load, and I graduated in only 3 semesters with a double major in computer science and mathematics. At graduation I was presented with special award given to the top computer science student. I was amazed at the powerful transformation I went through as a result of exposing myself to daily inspiration.

After graduating I started a computer games business and ran it for 10 years. For the first 5 years, it was a real struggle. I sank into debt and went bankrupt. But I didn't give up because I understood the value of persistence. I kept going and eventually turned the business around. For the next 5 years, it did very well. Our games won several awards, and we had a write-up and photo published in the New York Times.

As I began to appreciate the amazing payoffs from investing in personal growth, I devoured many more books in the field and eventually read more than 1000 of them. I listened to audio programs and went to seminars to keep learning and growing. Soon I was formulating my own insights to build upon this knowledge—and to connect the dots between what I'd learned from others and what I'd experienced for myself."

Do/did you have a similar story? Getting started and sticking to a new habit for a few weeks is hard, but once you overcome inertia, it gets easier with each repetition. You need to grasp that the change you are about to make is long-term, and that a daily commitment is required.

If you have read the entirety of this concise book, you are now aware of the challenges that lie ahead and the steps you can take to overcome them. The workbook in the following pages is a motivational guide to your goal accomplishments and personal improvement.

Be faithful to your personal growth. Set goals every day, track progress and never stop learning. The only person who can cheat you out of your destiny is yourself. Remember that multiverse I mentioned in the first chapter – which version do you want to be? The answer lies beyond these pages.

THE MONTAGE OF YOUR LIFE

"We'll never make it to our milestones if we can't make it through our moments"

-Beth Moore

Montages are a series of short video clips edited into a sequence to condense space, time and information in cinema. They are usually included in a film to portray the progress achieved by a character over a given amount of time. Five months of hard work can be summarized in an inspiring five-minute clip, keeping audiences at the edge of their seats and rooting for the hero to succeed

What people tend to forget is that a montage is only a representation (often misleading) of the amount of time and work needed to achieve results similar to those of the characters. The real work includes the moments when you don't see any changes in your life, but you still forge on. Moments when you feel discouraged.

Moments when you fail and try again, having become all the wiser. And moments when you finally make it and rejoice. All of those moments combined produce the milestones that you will look back on and smile. So decide now; what is your montage going to look like?

ALL OR NOTHING

"Put your heart, mind and soul into even your smallest acts. This is the secret of success"

-Swami Sivananda

Excellence is a habit. Not a single act. It should translate into even the way you dress, walk and talk. You can't flip it on and off like a switch. Excellence comes through realizing that even the small things add up over time

It surpasses ordinary standards, and becomes the new standard. Excellence is a continuously moving target that can only be pursued through actions of integrity, meeting all obligations and continuously improving in all spheres

Whenever we slacken our efforts towards anything, it always seems inconsequential, but in the grand scheme of things, it could very well be the tipping point.

THE SEED AND HARVEST

"Don't judge each day by the harvest you reap but by the seeds that you plant."

Robert Louis Stevenson

If you have been faithful thus far, you may have been noticing a few minor improvements in your life. Perhaps you noticed that your body measurements have begun to go down, or you have improved your spending habits, or you have become more efficient at executing goals

It is believed to take approximately three weeks to form new habits and break old ones. Congratulations for staying the course, but it's not over yet. It's natural to rejoice when you've accomplished your goals and achieved success, but success in itself is not final, nor is failure

We owe it to ourselves to continue to grow. There is always room for growth, and we must continue to strive to reach our potential. Growth doesn't mean more money, but better character, more knowledge and reaching out to others

Seek out more knowledge, improve your modulus operandi, and teach others what you have learnt. These are the seeds that we sow into the future.

WHATEVER IT TAKES

"If opportunity doesn't knock, build a door."

-Milton Berle

In this life, few opportunities come on a silver platter. Even fewer if you had allowed addiction into your life. They say that luck is when opportunity meets preparation, but what happens when you are prepared but no doors are opening for you? This is where persistence comes into play.

Have you ever seen grass growing through the cracks of a hard tennis court? It does so through three meters of concrete, asphalt and multiple rubberized layers. You can't take 'no' for an answer

Press on and do not let your enthusiasm fade with every failure. A close friend of mine got her dream job, after sending multiple resumes with no response, by giving the CEO a one-minute presentation of why he should hire her... in a parking lot

Stay true to yourself and persevere (just don't try anything that may warrant a restraining order)"You never know what's around the corner. It could be everything. Or it could be nothing. You keep putting one foot in front of the other, and then one day you look back and you've climbed a mountain"

LEGACY

"Someone is sitting in the shade today because someone planted a tree a long time ago."

-Warren Buffet

We cannot live forever; the only immortality we can hope to achieve in this life is to impact the generations to come and have our names etched in history. You may have faced challenges when you started out in life, but you can ensure that those who come after you don't have to

Whatever it is that you hope to achieve, always remember that it's bigger than you, and someone out there is counting on you to fulfill your destiny

Someone needs the job that you are going to create. Someone needs the inspiration that either your words or your life story will provide. Someone need s the inheritance that you will leave them, or the sizeable donation you will make to charity

It's a great big domino effect, and we owe it to ourselves to pay it forward. Reach out and touch forever.

NEVER TOO LATE

"It is never too late to be what you might have been."

- George Eliot

I want to ask you a very difficult question: would the child that you were be proud of the adult that you have become? If the ten-year-old you could see you now, what would they think? When I was ten I wanted to become a power ranger, but I knew that was unrealistic, so I had other hopes and dreams. As did you

Life happens, and most of us end up not having the life that we planned. It was probably beyond our control, and usually we blame our parents, the economy or politicians for stealing our dream away. But as long as you still draw in breath, it's never too late to pursue your dreams

You can still go to school, start practicing or audition for whatever it is you had given up on. People can say whatever they like, but you know what you want out of life and how to get there. Dust off that book of forgotten dreams and start flipping the pages again.

DARE TO TRY

"What great thing would you attempt If you knew you could not fail?"

-Robert H Schuller

Whenever we try to do something unconventional or scary, we tend to ask ourselves, "What if it fails?" We think about the embarrassment and the waste of time it would be if we don't succeed. Usually this results in either aiming for a fraction of the proposed outcomes, or giving up altogether in fear of failure. Instead of hoping for the best, we hope that it's not too bad

But what if you succeeded? What if you stopped aiming for singles, went for a homerun and knocked it out of the park? If it was guaranteed that you would succeed, what challenge would you take on?

We may not succeed all the time, but at least you will fall on the top of a mountain if you aim for the stars. Every great innovation we enjoy today were a result of people who dared to think out of the box and try. Other people said it wouldn't work, but they tried it anyway, because it just might. No risk, no reward.

NEVER GIVE UP

"Our greatest weakness lies in giving up. The most certain way to succeed is always to try just one more time"

Thomas A Edison

I remember watching a one-sided boxing match one Sunday afternoon. One of the fighters got pummeled repeatedly, and got acquainted with the mat more often than he would like. Every time the referee began the count, he rose up at count '7'.

"Are you alright? Do you want to continue?" the referee would ask, and the black-eyed boxer could barely nod in order to resume fighting. Eventually, in a surprising turn of events, the underdog won the fight by a knockout and emerged the victor

That fight taught me a valuable lesson: a successful man falls down nine times and succeeds on the tenth try. Winners never quit, quitters never win, and losers never even try

No matter how many times you fall down, get back up. You are not out for the count yet. You have got what it takes, but it will take everything you've got.

RUN YOUR OWN RACE

"The only person you should try to be better than, is the person you were yesterday"

-Unknown

I don't care who you are - whenever you reunite with people from your past - you can't help but take a snapshot of their life and compare it to your own. Maybe you just met an old schoolmate, or an ex- lover, but the fact that remains is that time has passed since you last met, and you're curious as to how your life holds up against theirs.

It's human nature. However, we should not use the lives of others as a yard stick for ours, because we all have a different purpose in this life. Picture life as an exam, and each and every one of us is given a different question paper. You cannot compare or copy your answer s from your neighbor because you all have different questions

You will only fuel insecurity if you compare your 'behind-the-scenes' with someone else's 'highlight reel' People will always have their best foot forward – especially those who know you. You have to live YOUR life and run your own race, staying within your lane and respecting other people's lanes.

BECOME A BETTER YOU

"To be yourself in a world that is constantly trying to change you is the greatest accomplishment"

-Ralph Waldo Emerson

As you continue to work on yourself and your goals, I sincerely hope that you are not trying to be like someone else, but rather trying to be a better you. Don't work on your body because you want to look like a catalogue model, or pursue a career path because you want to be the next (insert name here). Remember when I talked about running your own race? You can never be anyone else, but you can be a better version of yourself

You can be stronger, faster, healthier, wealthier, more efficient and more knowledgeable than you are now. You can make over your wardrobe, dress more meticulously, take good care of yourself and learn something new

Constantly work on improving yourself, and you would be surprised to find that there are actually people out there who admire you.

WHEN THE GOING GETS TOUGH...

"The harder the conflict, the more glorious the triumph."

- Thomas Paine

In his book, Words for Courageous Living, Neal Carson shares an interesting observation:

"A bar of steel worth $5 when made into horse shoes is worth $10If one takes the same bar of steel and makes it into needles it is worth $350. If it is made into pocket knife blades it is worth $32,000. But, if you take that $5 bar of steel and make it into springs for watches it is worth $250,000. Wow, what a difference a process makes!"

We all go through tough times - we don't choose to experience problems - but we can choose whether they make or break us. I'm sure a lot of people have at least once bought something using a crumpled note from their pocket or wallet. The note does not lose its value because it has been crumpled up, but it does if it gets torn. Do not let struggles tear you up, but stay strong and become all the better for it.

IT'S NEVER OVER

"Success is not final, failure is not fatal: it is the courage to continue that counts."

-Winston Churchill

One of three things has happened by now:

You have developed the habit of excellence and success in completing your goals and notice significant improvements in your lifestyle.

Your main objectives are huge, but you have achieved a little progress, and each week brings you a little closer to your dream.

You fell off the wagon somewhere along the line, or things did not work out as you planned and you don't see any change as yet.

In all three cases, I will say to you that your work is far from over. If you're improving, congratulations! But keep seeking opportunities to grow. If you're making baby steps, well, big shots are just little shots that kept shooting. And if you've failed, then pick yourself up and press on, forgetting what lies behind but remembering the lessons you've learnt.

UNWRAPPING TOMORROW, TODAY

"Yesterday is not ours to recover, but tomorrow is ours to win or lose."

   - Lindon B Johnson

Yesterday is gone, but we can still win back tomorrow by acting today. There is a Shona proverb that says, "Yesterday's meal will not comfort a crying baby" It means that the past cannot be changed, and thinking about it will not affect the present

We can reminisce about the past all day long – from wishing for the return of our glory days to regretting a mistake we could've avoided - and nothing will change in our lives

Just as time itself, we must move forward by transitioning from the present into the future. You may have had an undesirable past, but you chart a path towards a desirable future by acting now. Tomorrow is a gift that you begin to unwrap in the present. What will you see when you open it?

WHAT DO YOU SEE?

"It's not what you look at that matters, it's what you see."

Henry David Thoreau

Our default setting as human beings is to observe and not to perceive. The two words are often used interchangeably, but they do not necessarily mean the same thing. Observation entails gathering the facts, but perception searches deeper and looks for the truth.

Two people may observe the same thing, but they can perceive it differently. For example, you may look at a jagged wooden block and see a jagged wooden block, but to a carpenter, it can be a potential work of art. We are constantly bombarded with facts by the media, but it is up to us to see them as stumbling blocks or stepping stones.

Every entrepreneurial venture is founded on the principle of providing a solution to a problem and getting paid for it. Where others saw a problem, entrepreneurs saw a solution and an opportunity

Look in the mirror and tell me what you see. Is it a work of art waiting to be freed by chiseling out the rough edges, or just a regular 'block'?

DELAYED GRATIFICATION

"Don't give up what you want most for what you want now."

-Unknown

Delayed gratification, or deferred gratification, is the ability to resist the temptation for an immediate reward and wait for a later reward.

Generally, delayed gratification is associated with resisting a smaller but more immediate reward in order to receive a larger or more enduring reward later

Always leave room for fun and rewards, but do not bankrupt your future for 'cheap thrills'. Giving in to temptation is tantamount to eating your seed before you even plant it in the ground.

Be patient, exercise restraint, and the rewards will far outlast the premature pleasure. Muhammad Ali once said, "I hated every minute of training, but I said, 'Don't quit. Suffer now and live the rest of your life as a champion.'"

DESPAIR, HOPE AND ADAPTATION

"The pessimist complains about the wind; the optimist expects it to change; the realist adjusts the sails."

-Beth Moore

Problems usually arise when we least expect them. Complaining about them doesn't change anything, except draining you and those around you of the energy needed to tackle the situation

Hope and optimism are a good thing, but if they are accompanied by inaction, then all you will be is a happy person with a problem. Don't get me wrong; contentment is an admirable virtue, but it can quickly turn into complacency and stagnation

The only constant in this world is change, and we need to adapt in order to not only survive, but to thrive. You have been through a lot by now, and have no doubt experienced some obstacles in your goal – setting. Perhaps you've realized that you are more effective at night than during the day, or that your day job encroaches on your social time. Take note of these and adjust accordingly.

EYES ON THE PRIZE

"Obstacles are those frightful things you see when you take your eyes off your goal."

-Henry Ford

Horses have peripheral vision, which means they can end up running off course in a race, unless they are made to remain focused. Blinders are small squares of firm leather that attach to the bridle at the side of the horse's head.

Some say that blinders were invented when a preacher had a wager with one of his friends. The preacher bet that his horse could walk up the stairs in his home, which the horse did with no problem at all. But, when he tried to coax the horse down again, it wouldn't budge! So, the preacher covered the horses head and lead him down. He realized that covering all or part of the horse's vision could encourage the horse to take chances it would not normally take.

This is the same with us. When we take our eyes of the goal, we see the challenges surrounding it, and become afraid. This week, I encourage you to put your blinders on and focus on the prize.

EVERY SECOND COUNTS

"If you love life, don't waste time, for time is what life is made up of"

-Bruce Lee

You have the same 86,400 seconds a day that Michelangelo, Helen Keller, Thomas Jefferson and Albert Einstein had in their time. Think about that for a minute (if you can spare sixty seconds, that is).

Effective use of our time is key to success, and embracing every passing moment as it happens is key to happiness. Abraham Lincoln once suggested that we should divide our day into three parts:

- A third is reserved for working;

- Another third is for leisure, and

- One third should be dedicated to rest

I have found that not only do I get things done this way, but I also feel refreshed during playtime and I get enough rest to start a new day

www.ingramcontent.com/pod-product-compliance
Lightning Source LLC
Chambersburg PA
CBHW050611160726
48003CB00003B/1139